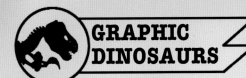

GRAPHIC DINOSAURS

presents

STEGOSAURUS

THE PLATED DINOSAUR!

ILLUSTRATED BY JAMES FIELD

BOOK HOUSE

Graphic Dinosaurs Stegosaurus
was produced by
David West Children's Books
7 Princeton Court
55 Felsham Road
London SW15 1AZ

Designed and written by Gary Jeffrey
Illustrated by James Field
Consultant: Steve Parker, Senior Scientific Fellow, Zoological Society of London
Cover designed by Rob Walker

First published in the UK in MMXII by Book House,
an imprint of The Salariya Book Company Ltd.,
25, Marlborough Place, Brighton BN1 1UB

Please visit the Salariya Book Company at:
www.book-house.co.uk

1 3 5 7 9 8 6 4 2

ISBN: 978-1-908177-73-5 (HB)
ISBN: 978-1-908177-46-9 (PB)

A CIP catalogue record for this book is available from the British Library.

Photographic credits: 5t, Postdlf, wikipedia project; 5r, AndonicO, en.wikipedia.org: 5b, Lee R. Berger; 30 (main), hibino, en.wikipedia.org, 30 (inset) Chris Gladis, en.wikipedia.org.

Printed and bound in China.

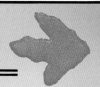

CONTENTS

WHAT IS A STEGOSAURUS?

STEGOSAURUS MEANS 'ROOF LIZARD'

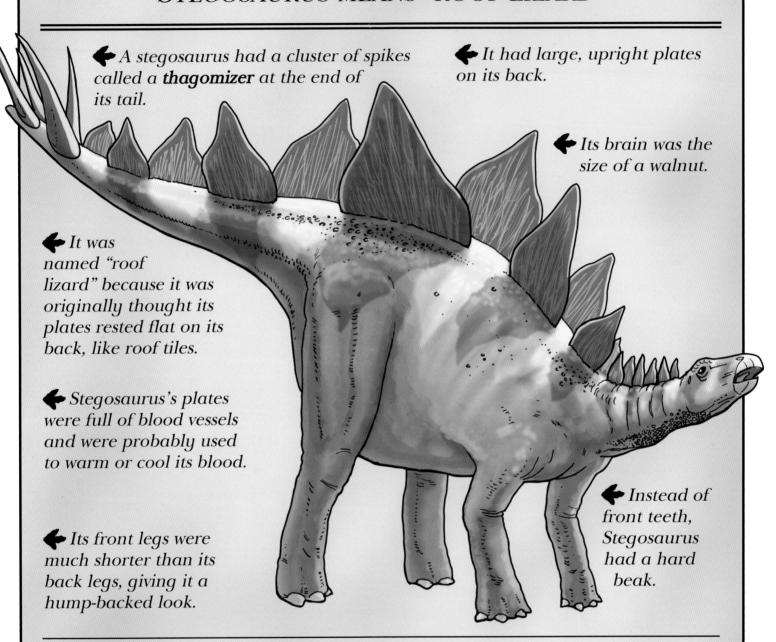

A stegosaurus had a cluster of spikes called a **thagomizer** at the end of its tail.

It had large, upright plates on its back.

It was named "roof lizard" because it was originally thought its plates rested flat on its back, like roof tiles.

Its brain was the size of a walnut.

Stegosaurus's plates were full of blood vessels and were probably used to warm or cool its blood.

Its front legs were much shorter than its back legs, giving it a hump-backed look.

Instead of front teeth, Stegosaurus had a hard beak.

STEGOSAURUS LIVED AROUND 160 MILLION TO 145 MILLION YEARS AGO, DURING THE JURASSIC PERIOD. FOSSILS OF ITS SKELETON HAVE BEEN FOUND IN NORTH AMERICA AND PORTUGAL (SEE PAGE 30).

Adult Stegosauruses measured up to 9 metres long, and 4 metres high to the top of the highest back plate. They weighed around 5,000 kilogrammes.

4

SMALL-BRAINED

A plaster cast was made of the inside of a Stegosaurus brain case. It was the size of a walnut, making it the smallest brain (in relation to body size) of any dinosaur. A larger cluster of nerves at the base of a Stegosaurus's spine may have acted like a second brain, helping it react quickly when attacked. Stegosaurus was as smart as it needed to be to **survive**.

A walnut at actual size.

PIECES OF A PUZZLE

The purpose of Stegosaurus's 17 plates is still a mystery. **Paleontologists** generally agree that they were too thin to have been used for armour. Being full of blood vessels, they may have reddened as a warning off sign to approaching attackers. The strong outline of the plates would also have helped Stegosauruses spot their own kind among other dinosaurs.

HEAT EXCHANGERS?

Just as African elephants' large ears help to cool their blood, Stegosaurus's back plates may have controlled its body temperature.

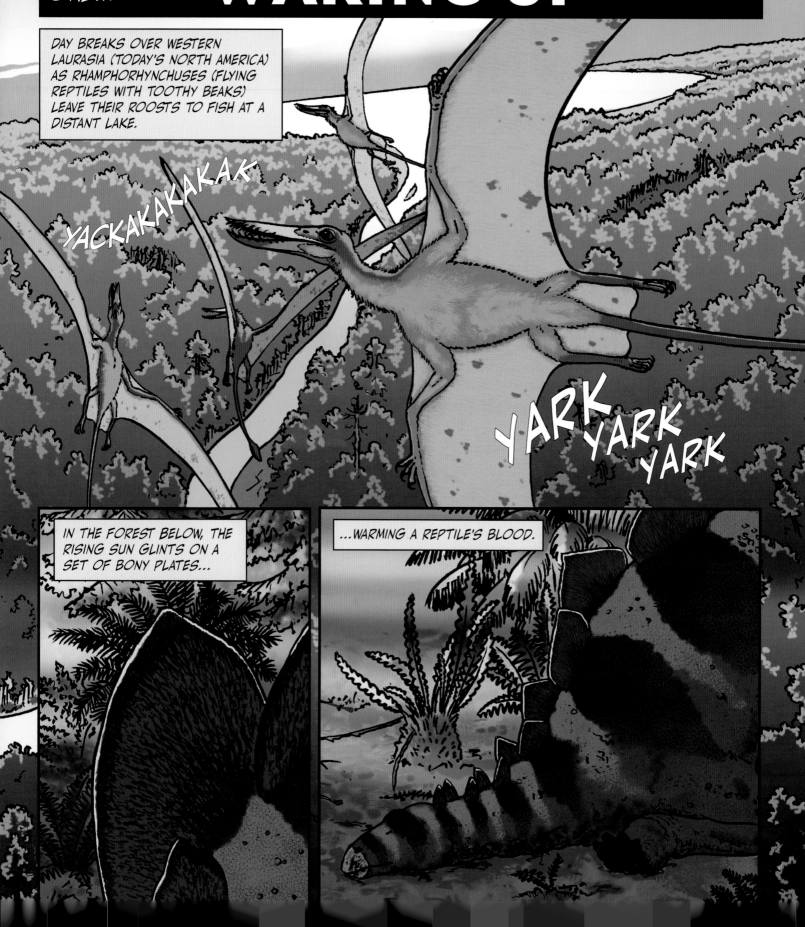

PART ONE... WAKING UP

DAY BREAKS OVER WESTERN LAURASIA (TODAY'S NORTH AMERICA) AS RHAMPHORHYNCHUSES (FLYING REPTILES WITH TOOTHY BEAKS) LEAVE THEIR ROOSTS TO FISH AT A DISTANT LAKE.

YACKAKAKAKAK

YARK YARK YARK

IN THE FOREST BELOW, THE RISING SUN GLINTS ON A SET OF BONY PLATES...

...WARMING A REPTILE'S BLOOD.

SHE YAWNS.

GWAAAAARGH

THE NOISE STARTLES A NEARBY FRUITAFOSSOR, A MAMMAL FEASTING ON SWARMING TERMITES.

SQUEEEEE

LIFTING HER HEAVY FRAME, THE **JUVENILE** STEGOSAURUS CALLS OUT TO THE ADULTS IN HER GROUP.

BWOAAAAAARK!

ALTHOUGH JUST THREE YEARS OLD, SHE IS ALREADY OVER 2 METRES LONG. HER CALL IS A DEEP BELLOW THAT SAYS "GET UP! IT IS TIME TO EAT!"

SQUEEEE SQUEEEE

IT IS THE DRY SEASON. THE GROUP FOLLOWS A BULL (OR MALE) TO FEED IN THE FORESTS THAT GROW ALONG A RIVER.

HERE THE PLANTS ARE LUSH, THEY BREAKFAST ON FIR LEAVES, FERNS, AND GIANT CYCADS.

THESE RIVER FORESTS ARE HOME TO ALL KINDS OF DINOSAURS. SMALL OTHNIELIAS RUSH IN TO PICK OVER THE DEBRIS LEFT IN THE STEGOSAURUSES' TRAIL.

THE JUVENILE STEGOSAURUS SNIFFS AT A CYCAD. IT IS VERY TEMPTING, BUT JUST OUT OF REACH.

SNUFFFLE SNIFF

WANTING A CHANGE FROM THE BORING, LOW-GROWING FERNS, SHE REARS UP.

DELLWHUP

SHE IS UNAWARE...

...THAT SHE IS BEING WATCHED.

THE PREDATOR EMERGES. IT IS A CERATOSAURUS, A FIERCE MEAT EATER. HIS JAWS ARE STRONG ENOUGH TO CAUSE A SERIOUS WOUND.

GRRRAAAGH

THE OTHNIELIAS PANIC.

GLAAAAARRRKK

THE STEGOSAURUS CRIES OUT IN ALARM...

GWEEEEEEEE

...BUT TODAY SHE IS NOT THE PREY.

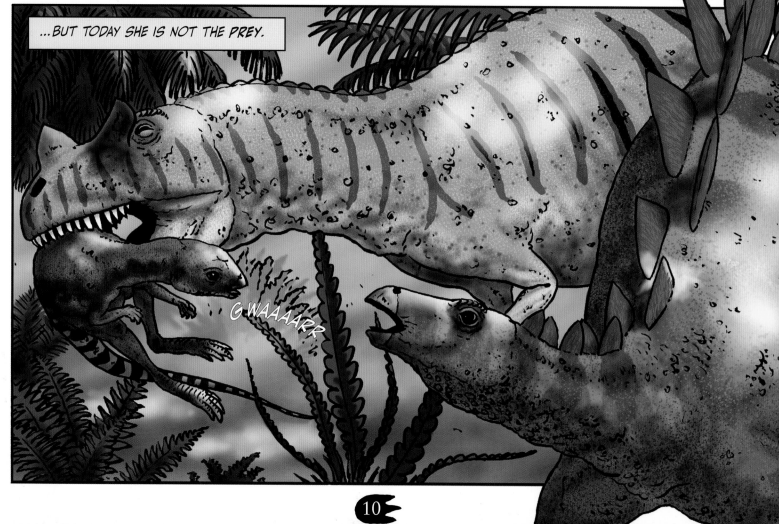

GWAAAARR

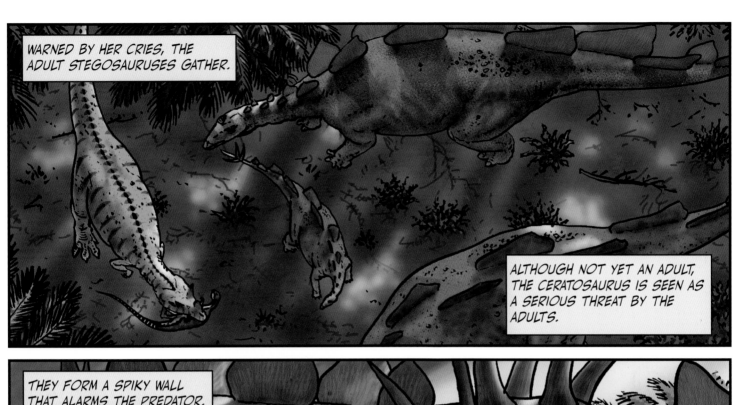

WARNED BY HER CRIES, THE ADULT STEGOSAURUSES GATHER.

ALTHOUGH NOT YET AN ADULT, THE CERATOSAURUS IS SEEN AS A SERIOUS THREAT BY THE ADULTS.

THEY FORM A SPIKY WALL THAT ALARMS THE PREDATOR.

THE CERATOSAURUS STALKS OFF TO EAT HIS PRIZE IN PEACE.

THE FOREST IS QUIET AGAIN. WHILE THE ADULTS CONTINUE FEEDING, THE JUVENILE STEGOSAURUS PRACTISES SWINGING HER TAIL SPIKES.

INSPIRED BY THE ADULTS' EARLIER DISPLAY, SHE FLEXES HER TAIL MUSCLES...

...WHICH ARE ALREADY...

BOK!

...QUITE STRONG.

CRRRACCK!

MWAAARGH

A PIECE OF ROTTEN WOOD IS STUCK ON HER SPIKES. SHE TRIES TO SHAKE IT OFF.

SHE FLEXES HER TAIL FOR A MIGHTY SWING AT THE TREE TRUNK.

KRACK!

HER BONY THAGOMIZER, AS SHARP AS A PICKAXE, MAY ONE DAY SAVE HER LIFE.

IN THE HEAT OF THE DAY, THE STEGOSAURUSES HAVE MADE THEIR WAY TO THE LAKE.

THE DRY SEASON HAS BEEN LONG-LASTING. THE LEVEL OF THE LAKE IS DOWN. AN OVERHEATED APATOSAURUS IS MAKING THE MOST OF THE LOW WATER.

THE AREA IS FULL OF OTHER SAUROPODS, SUCH AS BRACHIOSAURUSES, WHO GRAZE THE HIGH TREETOPS THAT LINE THE EDGES OF THE WATERING HOLE.

A JUVENILE CAMARASAURUS BLOCKS THE WAY TO THE WATER.

THE JUVENILE STEGOSAURUS CHALLENGES THE YOUNG SAUROPOD. 'MOVE BACK!' SHE GROWLS.

GWAAAAARRRK!

THE CAMARASAURUS IS FRIGHTENED BY THE SPIKY NEWCOMER AND TAKES OFF...

GWEEEEEEEK

...BACK TO ITS PARENT.

GWEEEK GWEEK

THE ADULT CAMARASAURUS RESPONDS TO THE THREAT BY RAISING ITS BIG CLAWED FOOT...

BROOAARRGH

...AND MOVING IN.

RRRAAAGH

BOOM

THE JUVENILE IS ABOUT TO BE TRAMPLED.

GWEEEP!

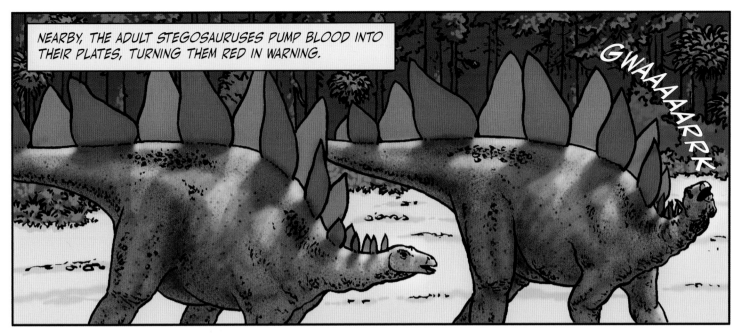

NEARBY, THE ADULT STEGOSAURUSES PUMP BLOOD INTO THEIR PLATES, TURNING THEM RED IN WARNING.

GWAAAAARRK

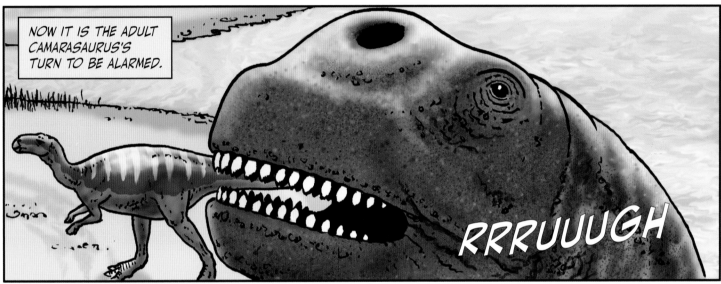

NOW IT IS THE ADULT CAMARASAURUS'S TURN TO BE ALARMED.

RRRUUUGH

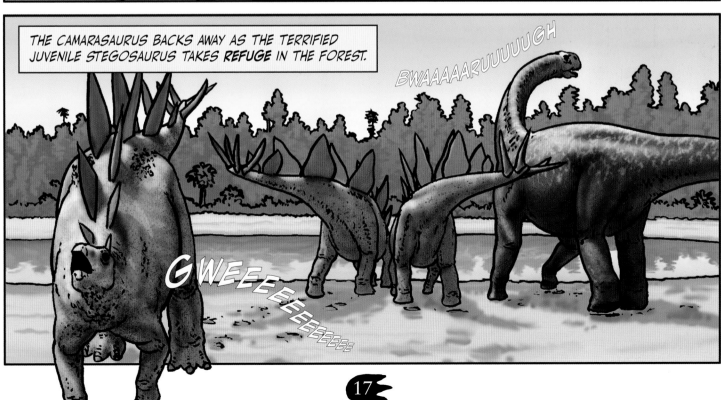

THE CAMARASAURUS BACKS AWAY AS THE TERRIFIED JUVENILE STEGOSAURUS TAKES **REFUGE** IN THE FOREST.

BWAAAAARUUUUUGH

GWEEEEEEEEGGG

AN ORNITHOLESTES IS ATTACKING AN ABANDONED CAMPTOSAURUS'S NEST.

BZZZZZZZZZZZ

GLUMMMMNGH

THE STEGOSAURUS'S ATTENTION IS ON THE NEST ROBBER, SO SHE FAILS TO NOTICE THAT SOMETHING HAS SLIPPED INTO THE WATER BEHIND HER...

GWOOOOP

...AND IS MOVING TOWARD HER.

GWEEEP

A CERATOSAURUS LEAPS FROM THE WATER...

BORAAAAAGH!

...BUT, YET AGAIN, THE STEGOSAURUS...

...IS NOT THE PREY.

FEARING ATTACK, SHE TURNS TO LEAVE THE FOREST...

...BUT THE WAY AHEAD IS BLOCKED...

...BY AN ALLOSAURUS!

GWRRRRRRRRRR

21

AS SHE TURNS TO CHECK ON THE CERATOSAURUS, HE DROPS THE ORNITHOLESTES AND COMES AFTER HER.

BOOOUWAAAGH

HOLDING HER GROUND, SHE SWISHES HER TAIL SPIKES AT HER ATTACKER...

...BUT THE CERATOSAURUS KEEPS COMING.

GRRRAAAAGH

SHE HAS NO CHOICE. SHE MUST RUN PAST THE ALLOSAURUS.

AS THE ALLOSAURUS DRINKS...

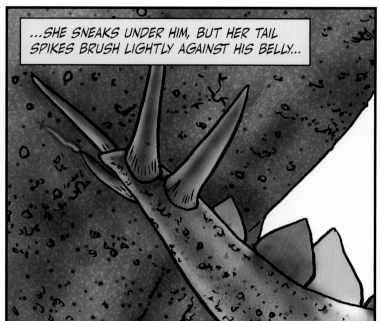

...SHE SNEAKS UNDER HIM, BUT HER TAIL SPIKES BRUSH LIGHTLY AGAINST HIS BELLY...

...ALERTING HIM THAT SHE'S THERE.

GRRRAAGH

THE ALLOSAURUS CHASES HER.

GRRAAH

DOUFFF

HE IS EXCITED BY THE THOUGHT OF MORE FRESH MEAT.

SPLOSH!

GRRRRRRRRRRRRRRRR

THE ALLOSAURUS IS WEIGHED DOWN BY HIS RECENT MEAL.

BWAARK

THE STEGOSAURUS REACHES THE SAFETY OF HER GROUP.

GRRRRRRRRRRRRRR

THE BULL STEGOSAURUS HOLDS HIS GROUND. THE PREDATOR IS TOO CLOSE TO OUTRUN NOW.

BWAARK

25

PART FOUR

DEATH MATCH

THE ALLOSAURUS HAS BACKED THE STEGOSAURUS INTO THE LAKE, SCATTERING A GROUP OF DRYOSAURUSES.

THE PREDATOR ATTACKS. BEHIND IT FRIGHTENED DRYOSAURUSES TAKE COVER.

BOURAAAAGH!

SPINNING ON HIS HIND LEGS, THE STEGOSAURUS DESPERATELY TWISTS AWAY...

...TRYING TO AVOID THE ALLOSAURUS'S RIPPING CLAWS.

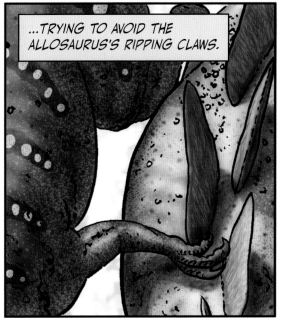

MEANWHILE HE THRASHES HIS THAGOMIZER TOWARD THE ALLOSAURUS'S BACK.

BRRAAAAAGH!

KRACCCK

IT STRIKES!

THE BLOW TEARS INTO THE MEAT EATER'S FLESH AND CAUSES MASSIVE BLEEDING.

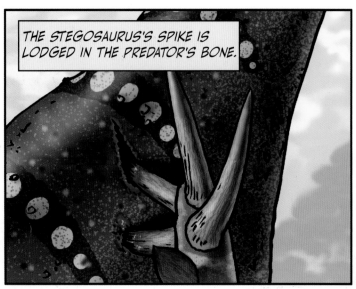

THE STEGOSAURUS'S SPIKE IS LODGED IN THE PREDATOR'S BONE.

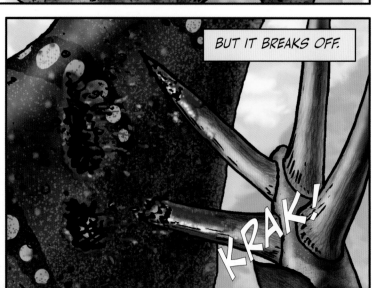

BUT IT BREAKS OFF.

KRAK!

THE GROUP MOVES OFF, LEAVING THE ALLOSAURUS TO ITS FATE.

GRRRRAAAAAAAAGH

GWEEEP

THE BULL HAS LOST PART OF A TAIL SPIKE, BUT HE WILL LIVE TO FIGHT ANOTHER DAY...

...UNLIKE THE ALLOSAURUS.

AS THE STEGOSAURUSES HEAD TOWARD THE FOREST, THE SKY DARKENS. THE WET-SEASON RAINS ARE COMING.

GWAAAARF!

THE LITTLE STEGOSAUR WILL SLEEP WELL TONIGHT.

29

FOSSIL EVIDENCE

WE CAN GET A GOOD IDEA OF WHAT DINOSAURS MAY HAVE LOOKED LIKE FROM THEIR FOSSILS. FOSSILS ARE FORMED WHEN THE HARD PARTS OF AN ANIMAL OR PLANT BECOME BURIED AND THEN TURN TO ROCK OVER MILLIONS OF YEARS.

Paleontologists think that the Stegosaurus's thagomizer (see inset below) might have been used as a defensive weapon. In 2005, a Stegosaurus neck plate was shown to have bite marks that matched the teeth pattern of an Allosaurus. An Allosaurus backbone had a hole in which a Stegosaurus thagomizer fitted perfectly. Over the years, many of the fossil thagomizers that have been dug up have had broken tips. This suggests that Stegosauruses and Allosauruses did indeed fight with each other, as shown in so many reconstructions (below).

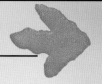

DINOSAUR GALLERY

ALL THESE DINOSAURS APPEAR IN THE STORY.

Othnielia
'For Othniel'
Length: 1.5 metres
A small, birdlike dinosaur named after famed fossil hunter Othniel Charles Marsh.

Ornitholestes
'Bird robber'
Length: 2 metres
A small, active meat eater with long forearms, which may have eaten eggs.

Dryosaurus
'Oak lizard'
Length: 3–4 metres
A small-to-medium-sized plant eater with unusual oak-leaf-shaped teeth.

Camptosaurus
'Bent lizard'
Length: 8 metres
A heavy-set plant eater that probably walked on four legs, but could raise itself up on two legs to reach food.

Ceratosaurus
'Horned lizard'
Length: 6–8 metres
A large meat eater with a big nose horn and bony crests in front of its eyes. It also had a thick tail like a crocodile and may have been a good swimmer.

Allosaurus
'Different lizard'
Length: 8.5–13 metres
A large meat eater with strong front claws. It was at the top of the late Jurassic food chain.

Camarasaurus
'Chambered lizard'
Length: 18 metres
A giant, strongly-built plant eater that had nostrils in front of and above its eyes.

GLOSSARY

cycads	Fernlike evergreen plants that have short, fat trunks.
fossils	The remains of living things that have turned to rock.
Jurassic period	The period of time between 200 million and 145 million years ago.
juvenile	Not fully grown.
paleontologists	Scientists who study fossils.
prey	Animals that are hunted for food by another animal.
refuge	Protection.
survive	To stay alive.
thagomizer	A Stegosaurus's tail spikes.

INDEX

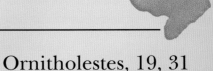